Mr. Longneck Coloring Book

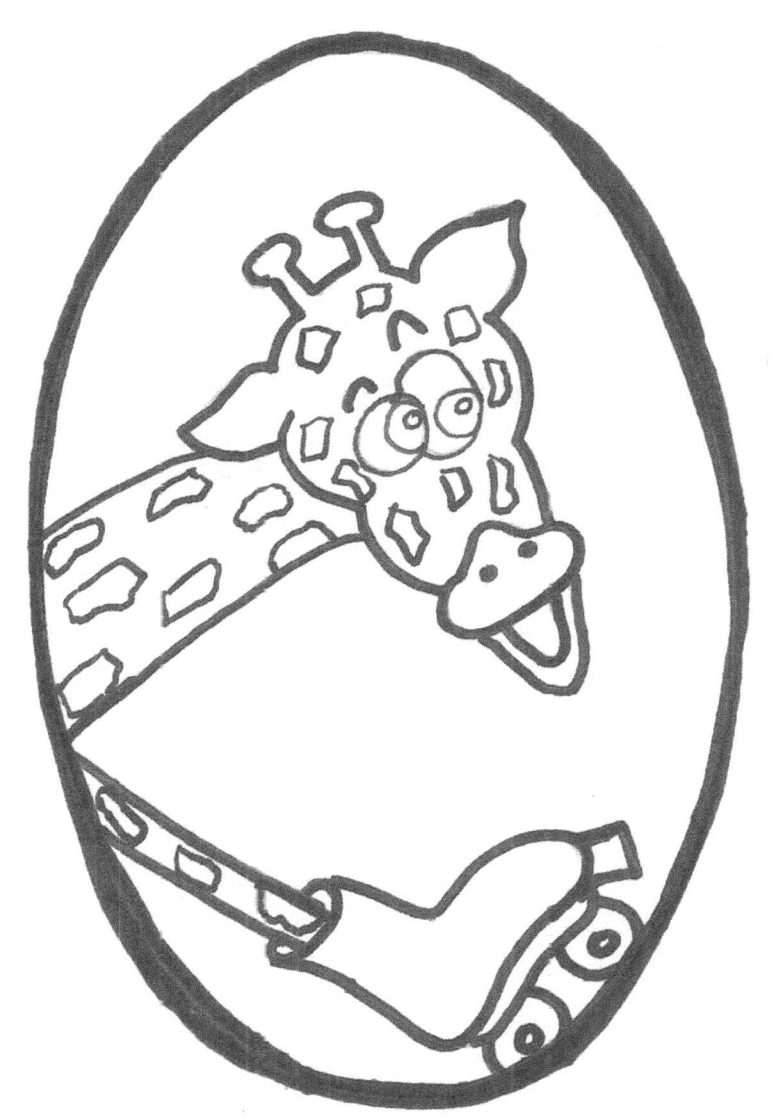

K.C. Gardner

Copyright © 2018 K.C. Gardner
All Rights Reserved
ISBN - 13:978-1719024600
ISBN-10:171902460X

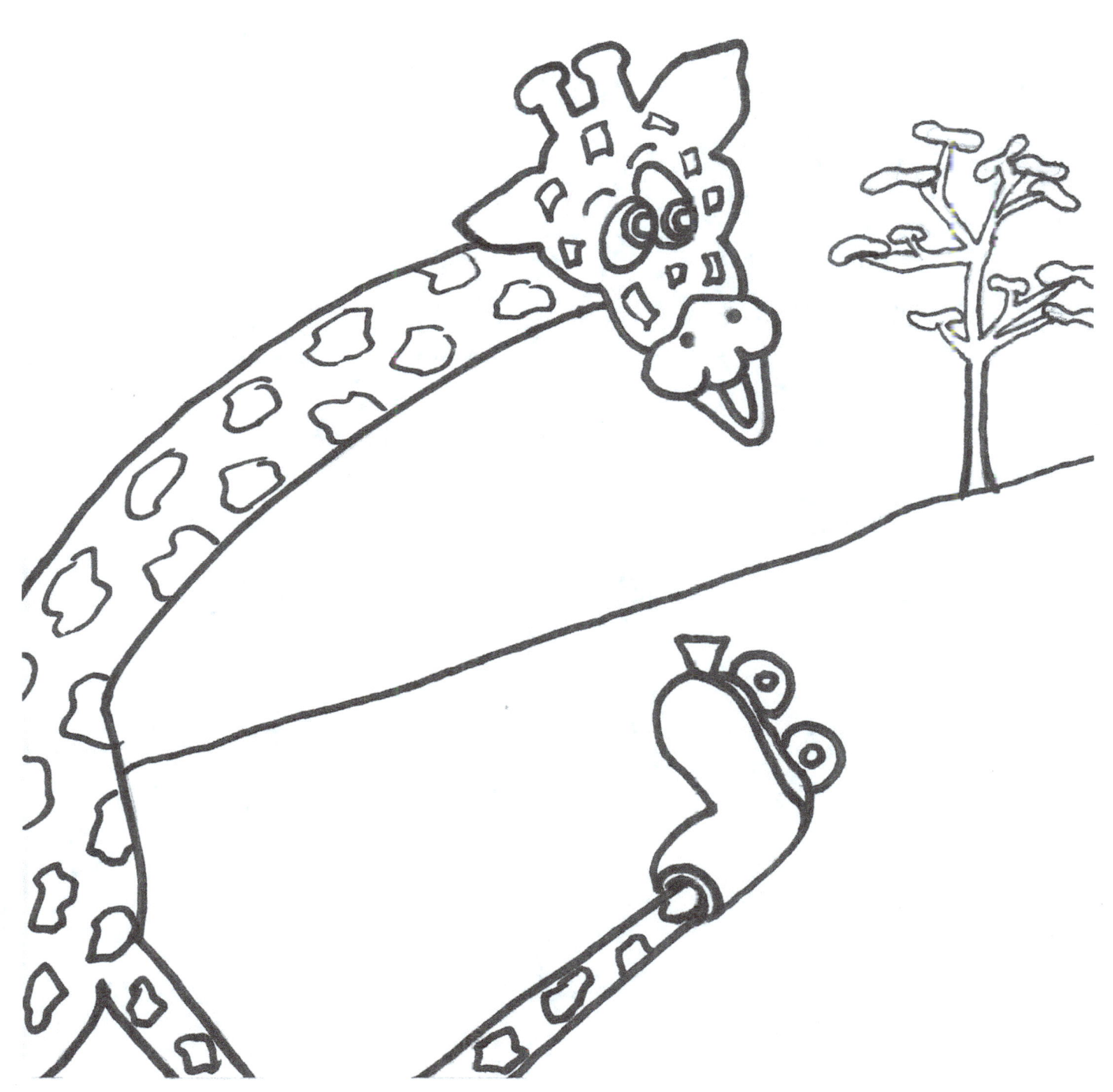

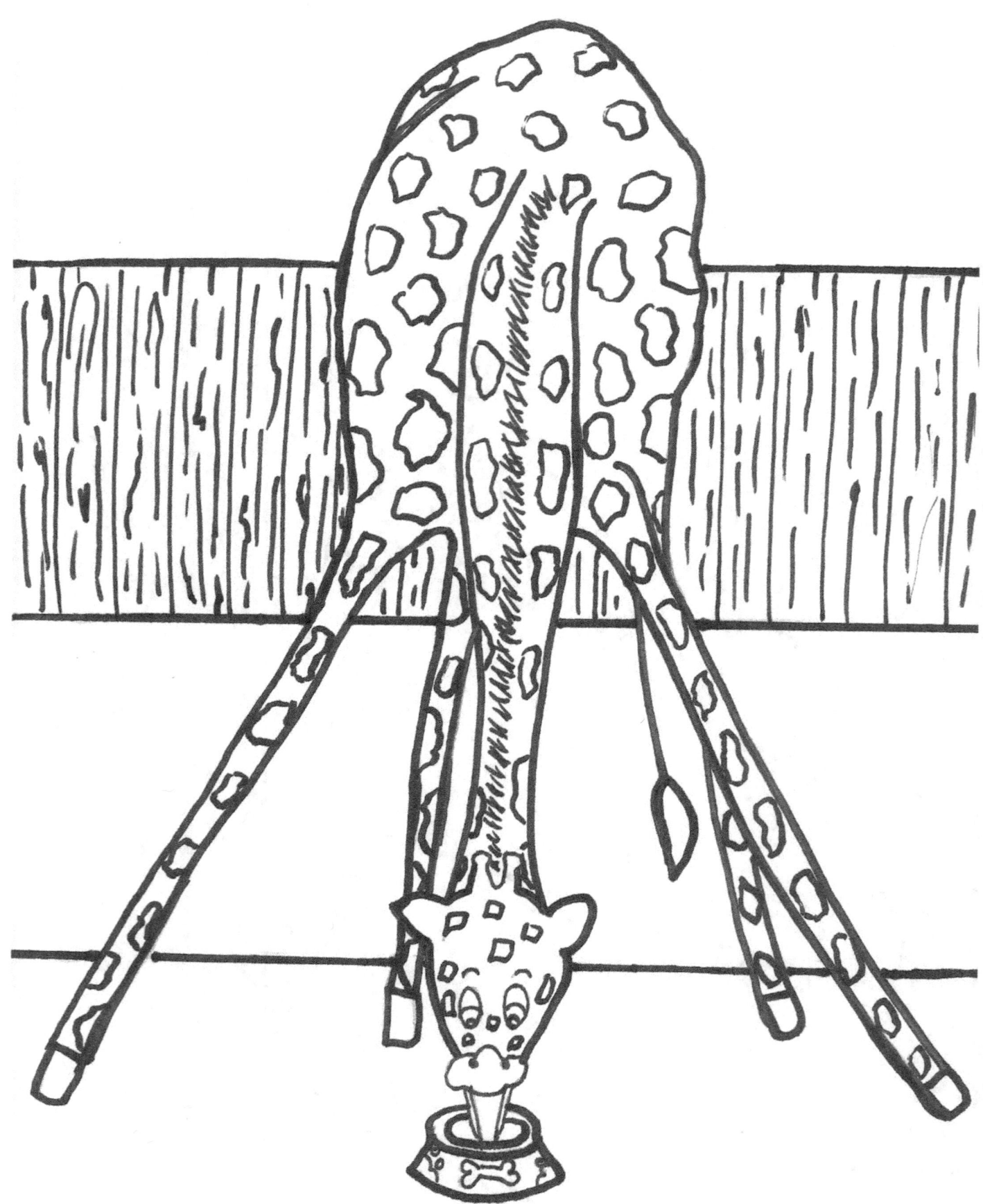

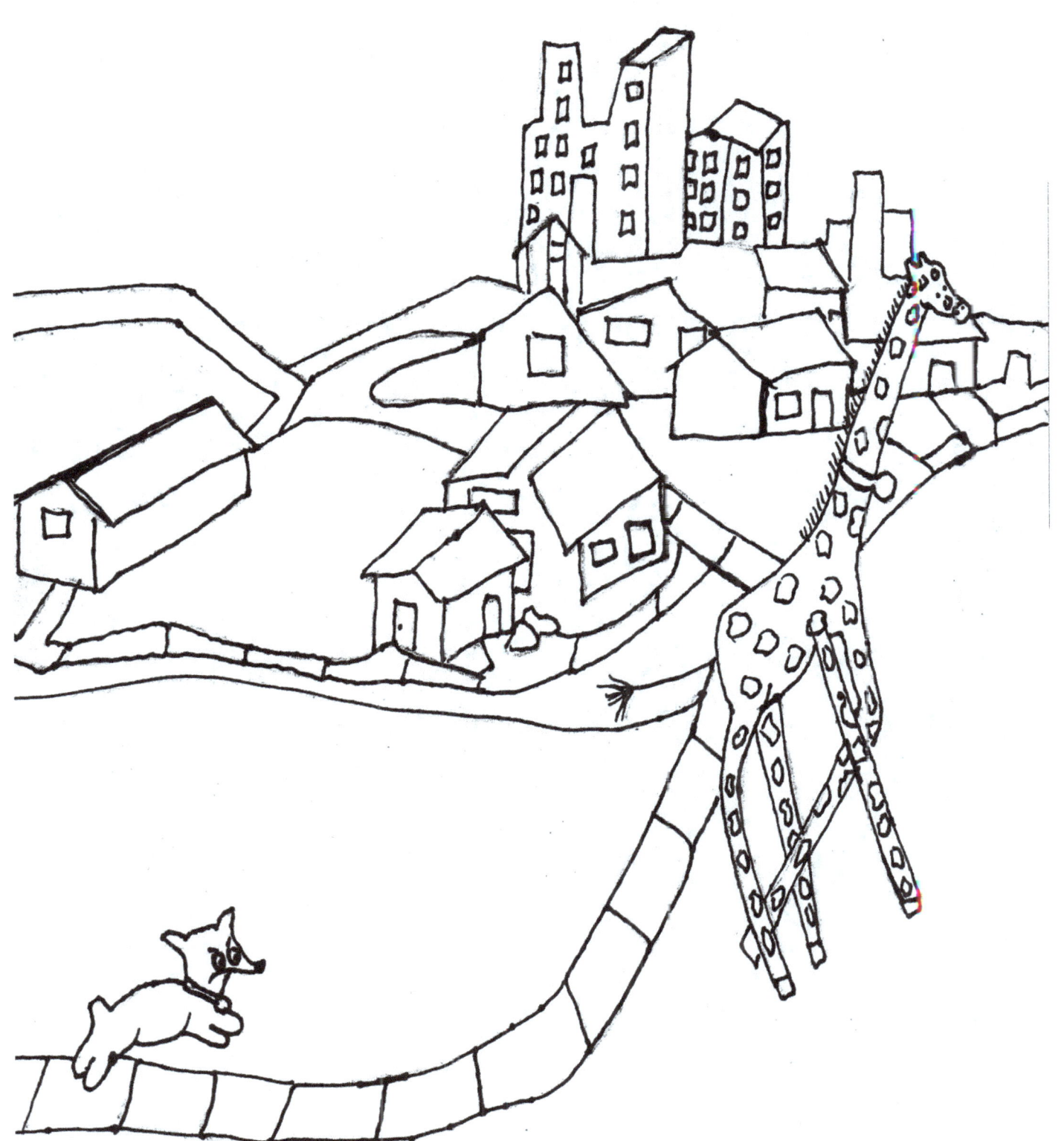

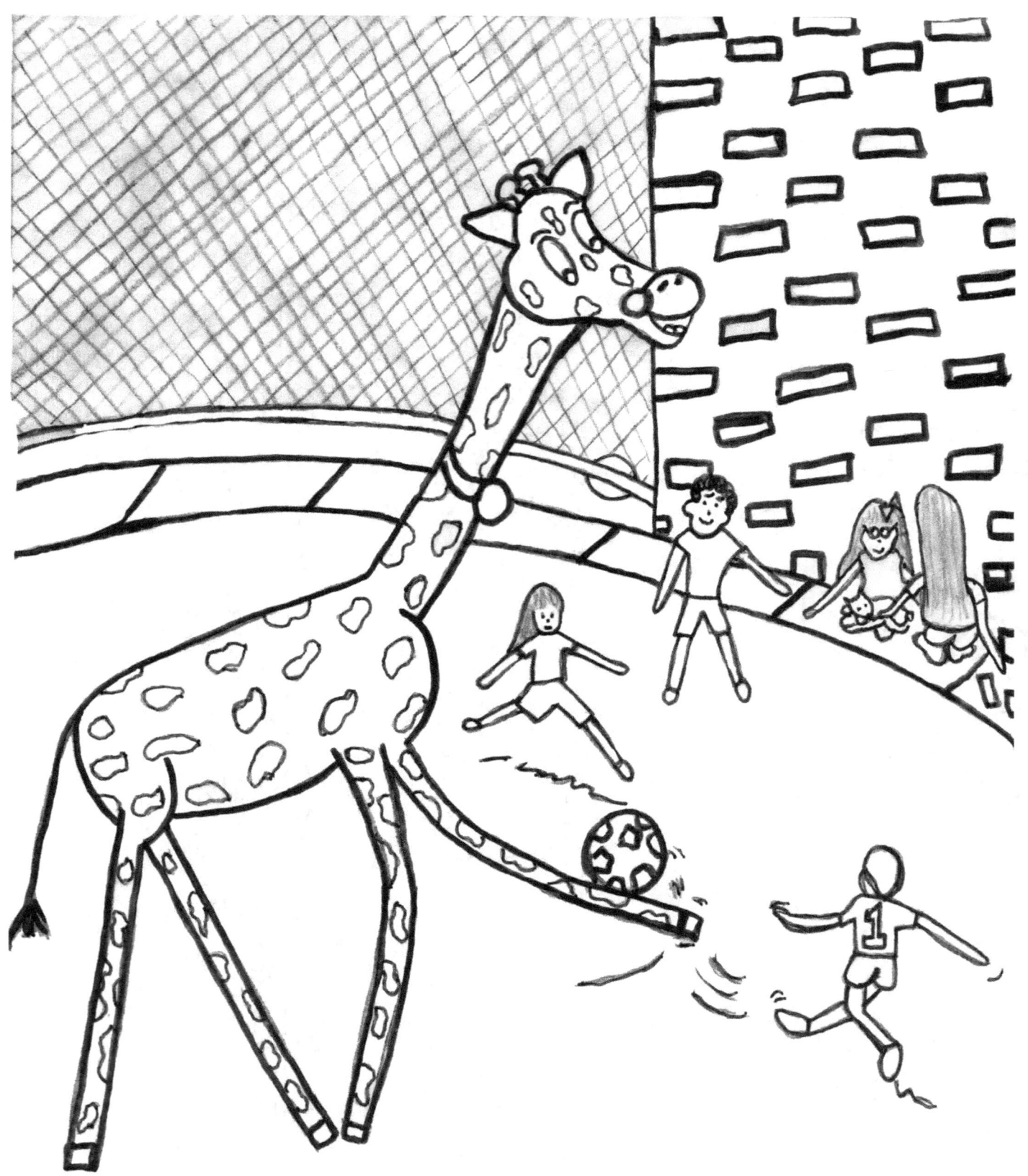

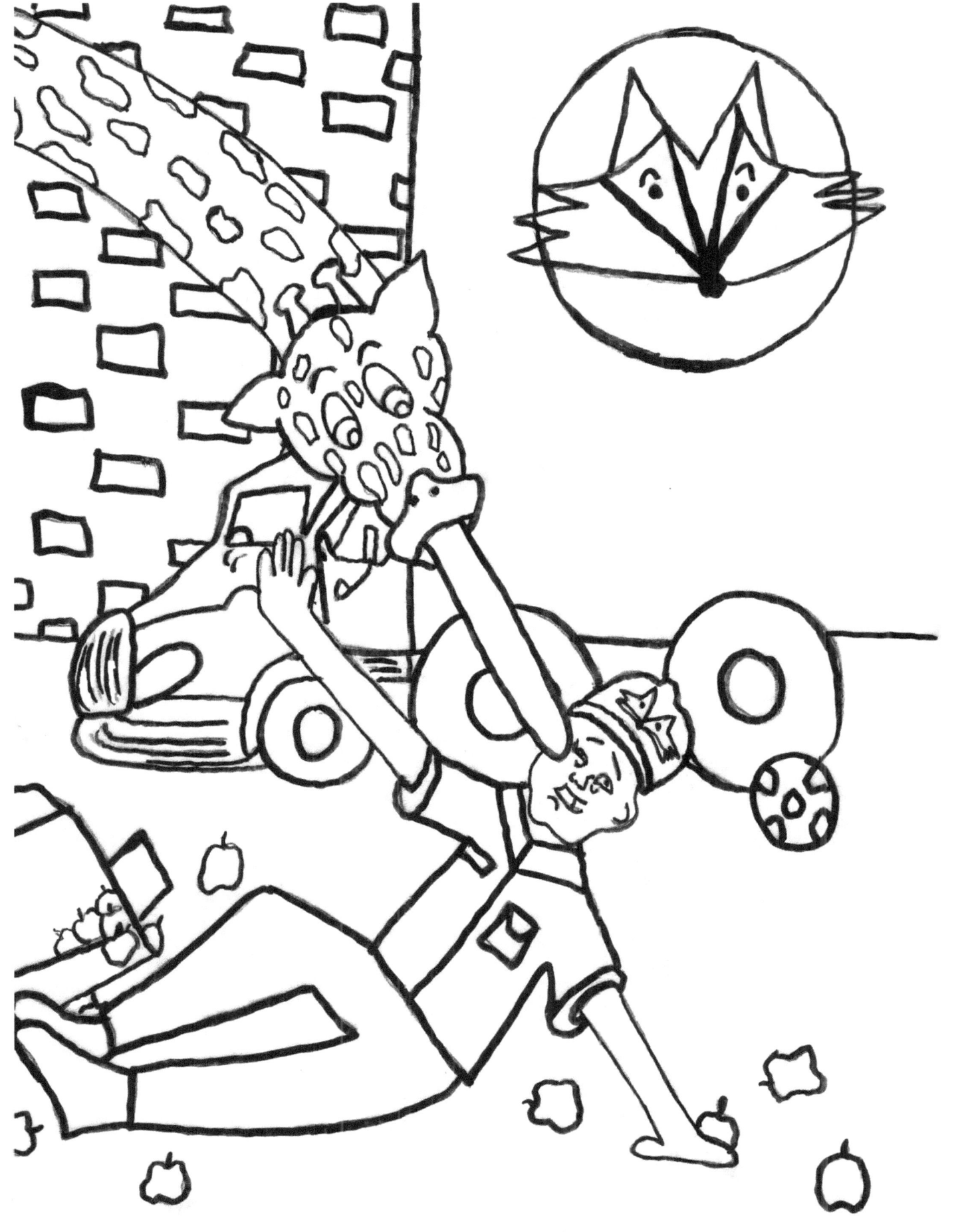

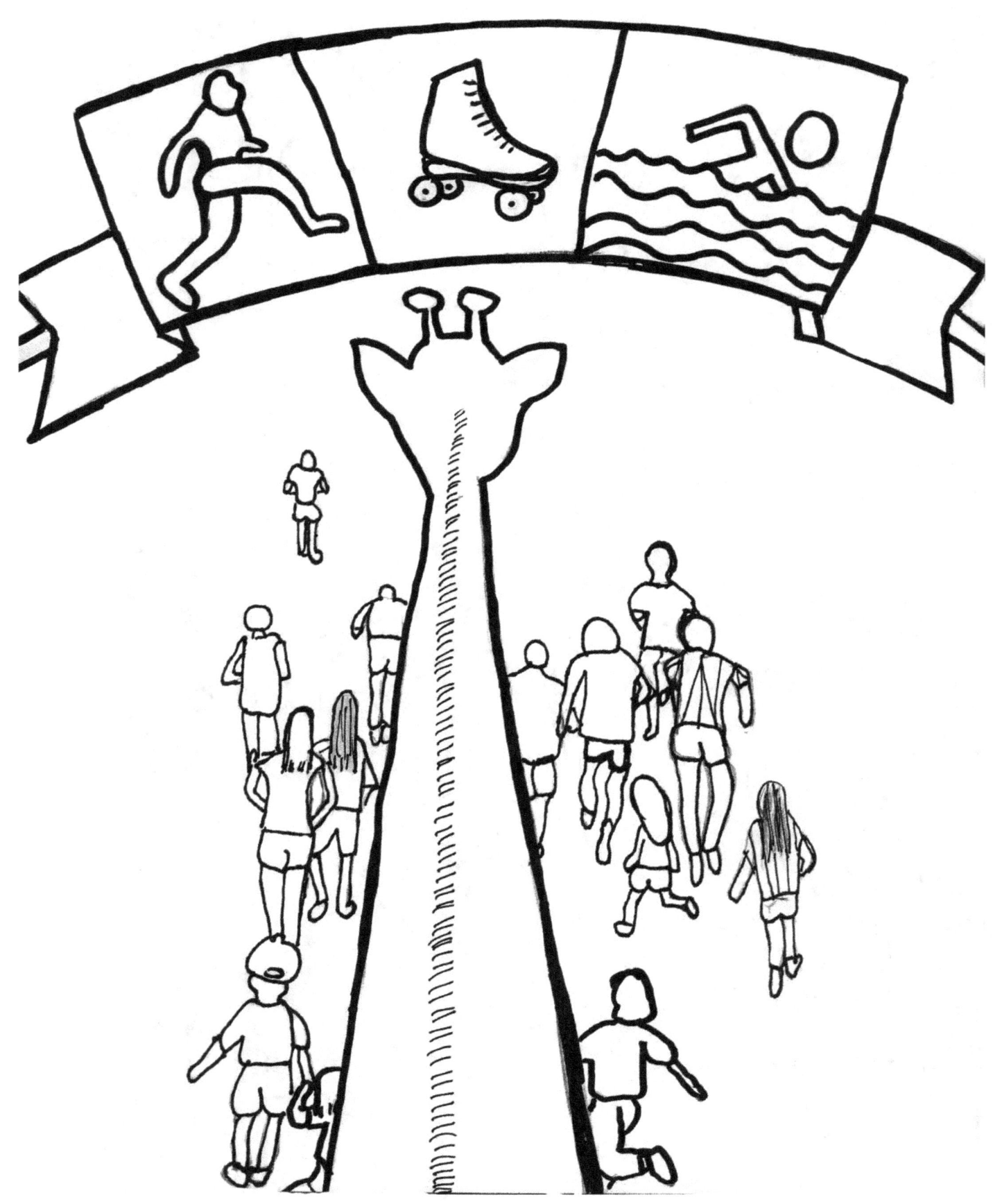

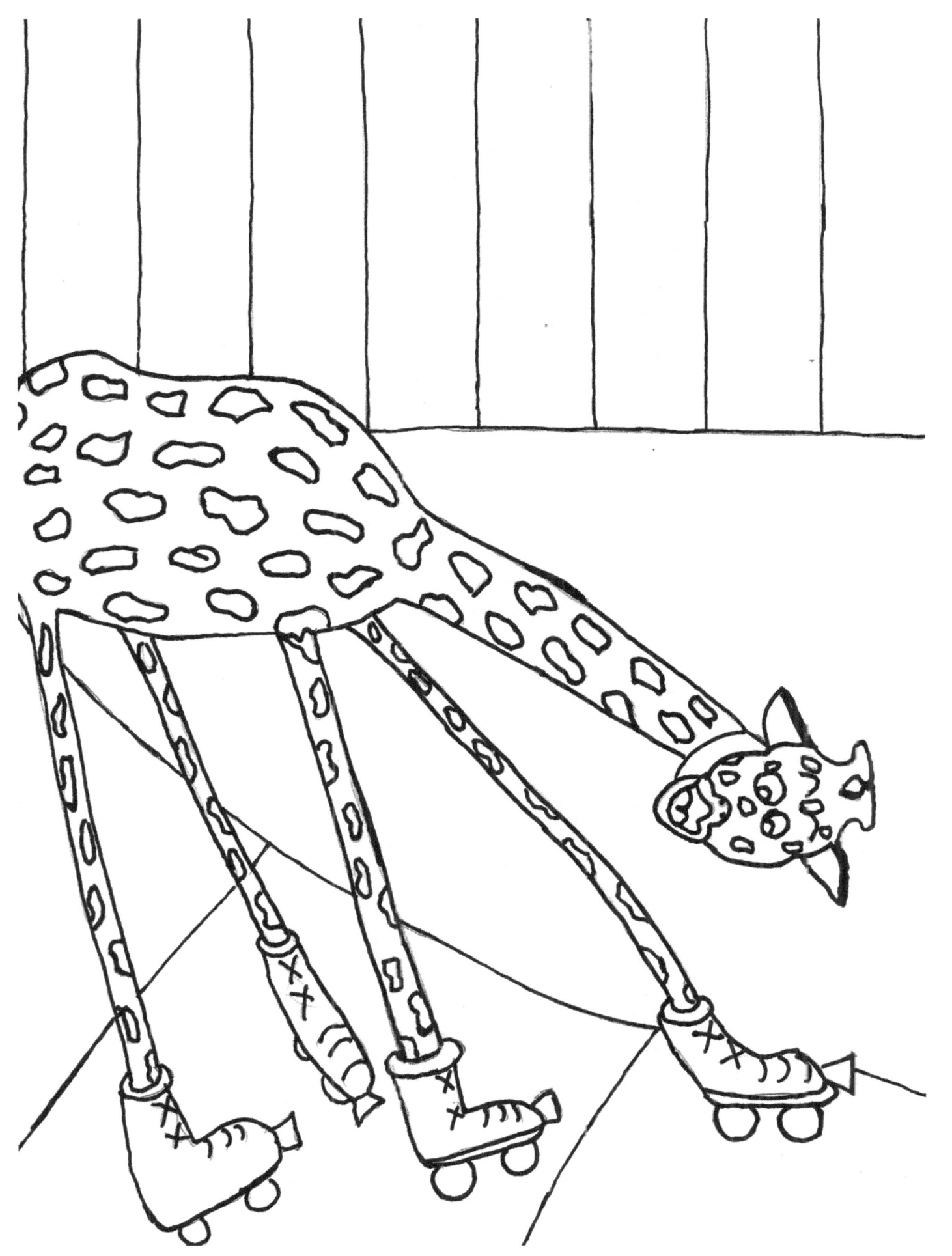

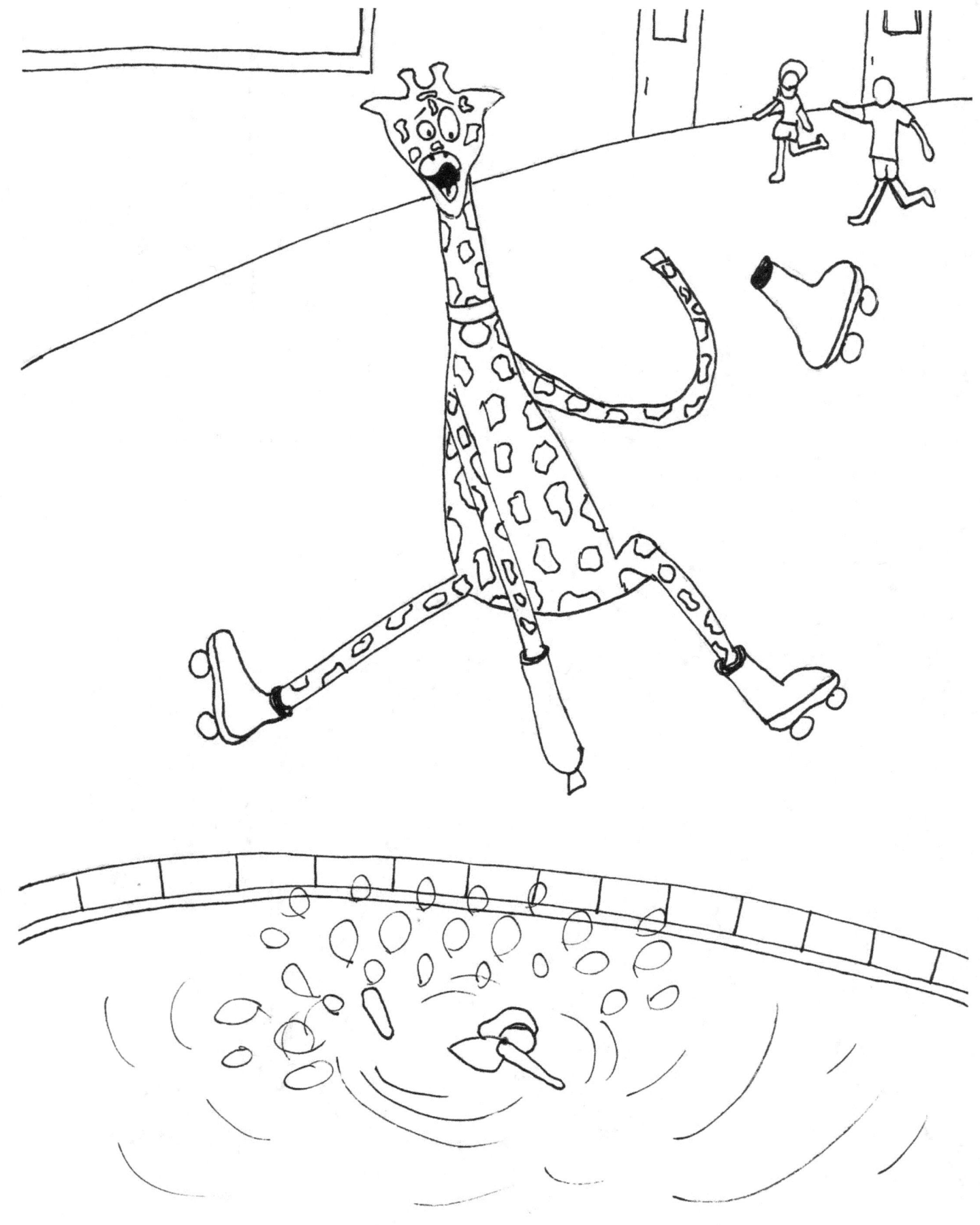

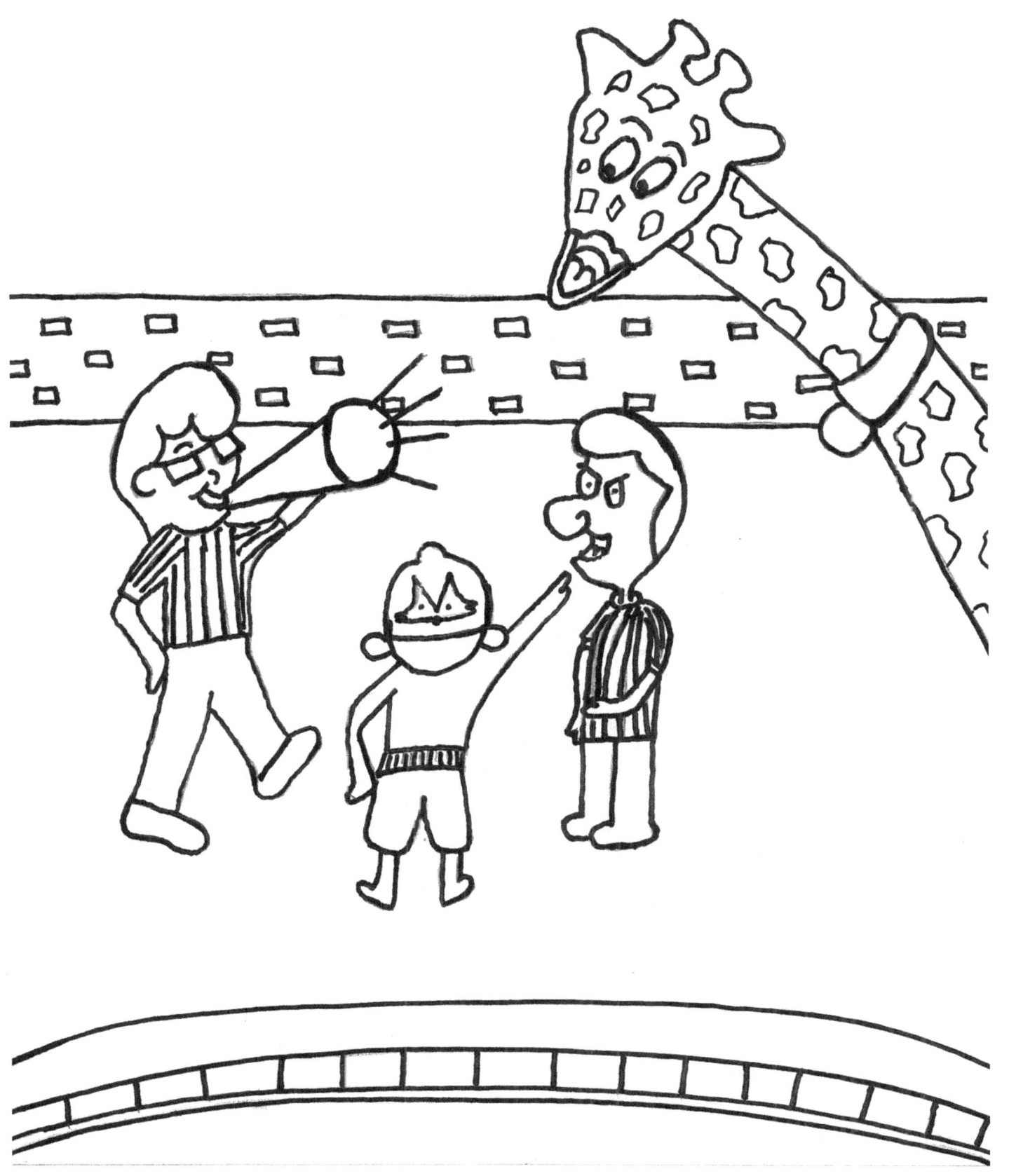

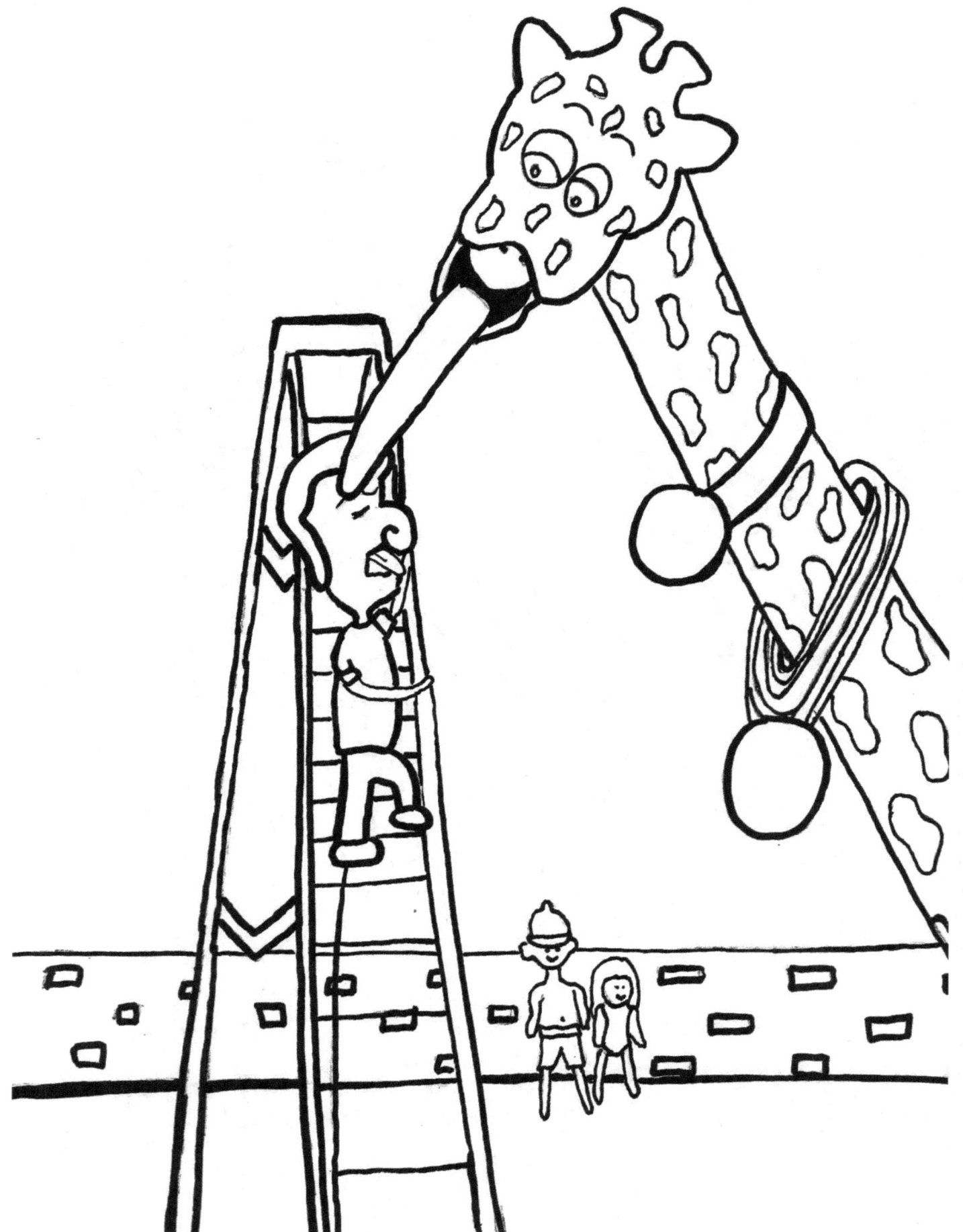

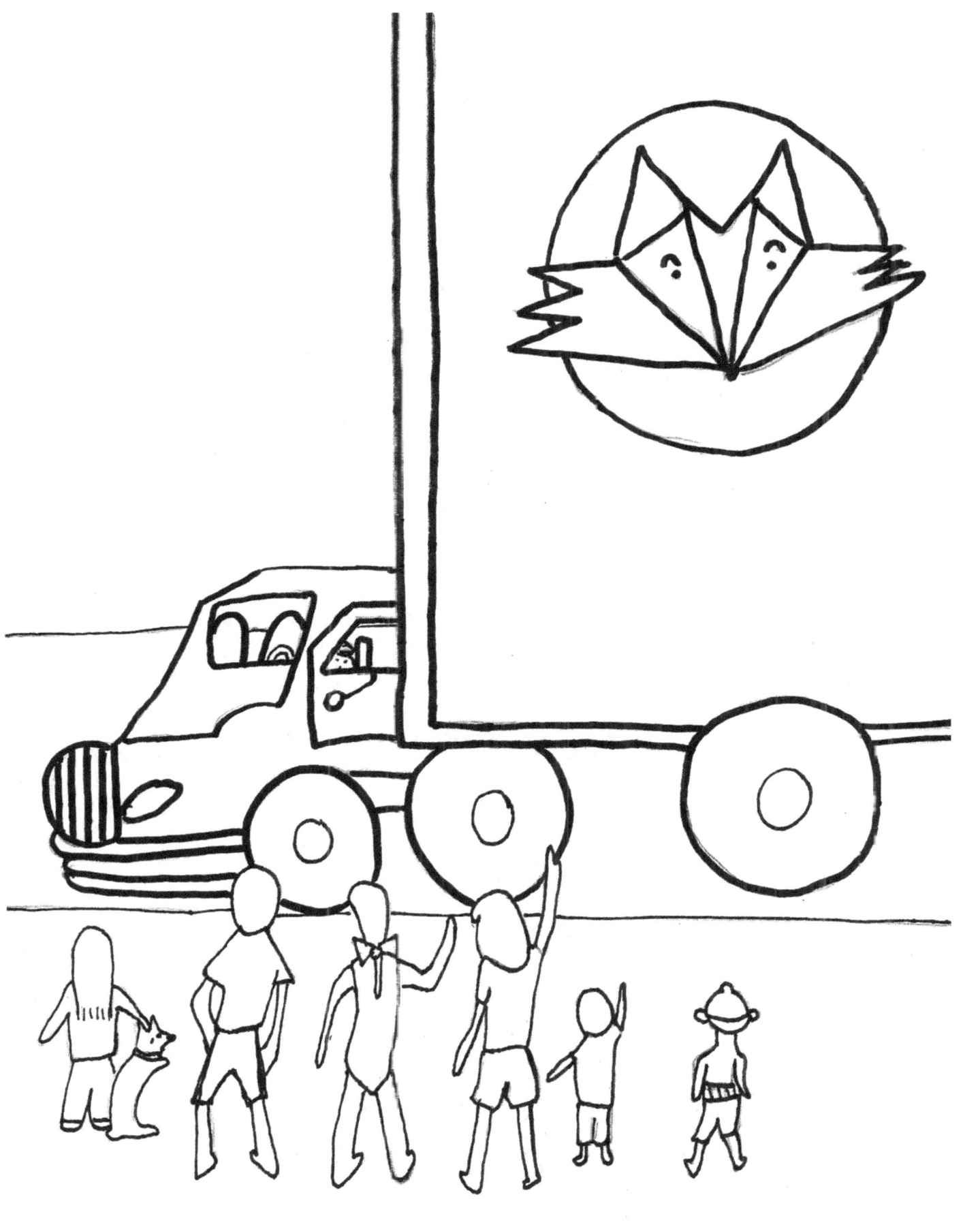

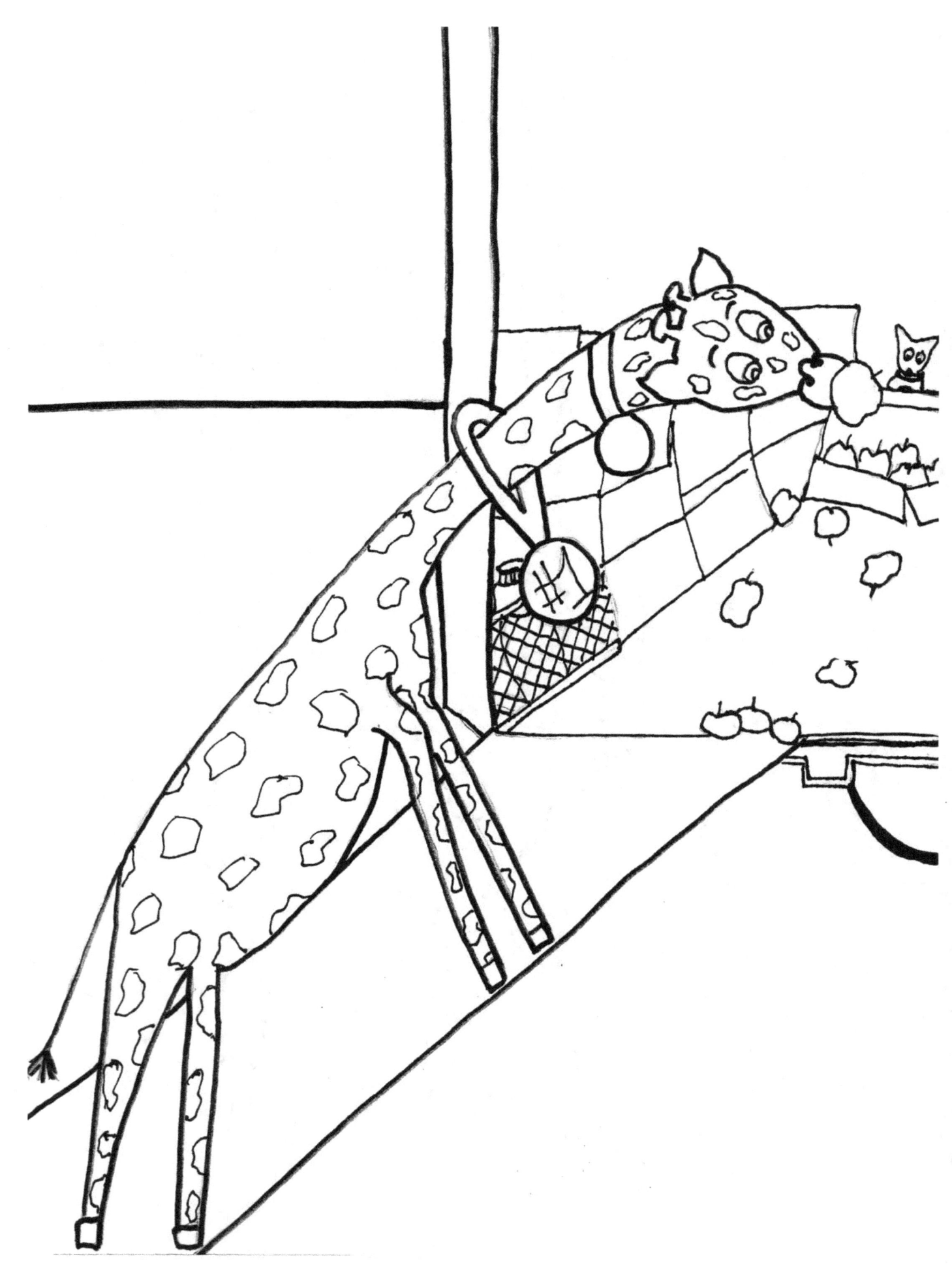

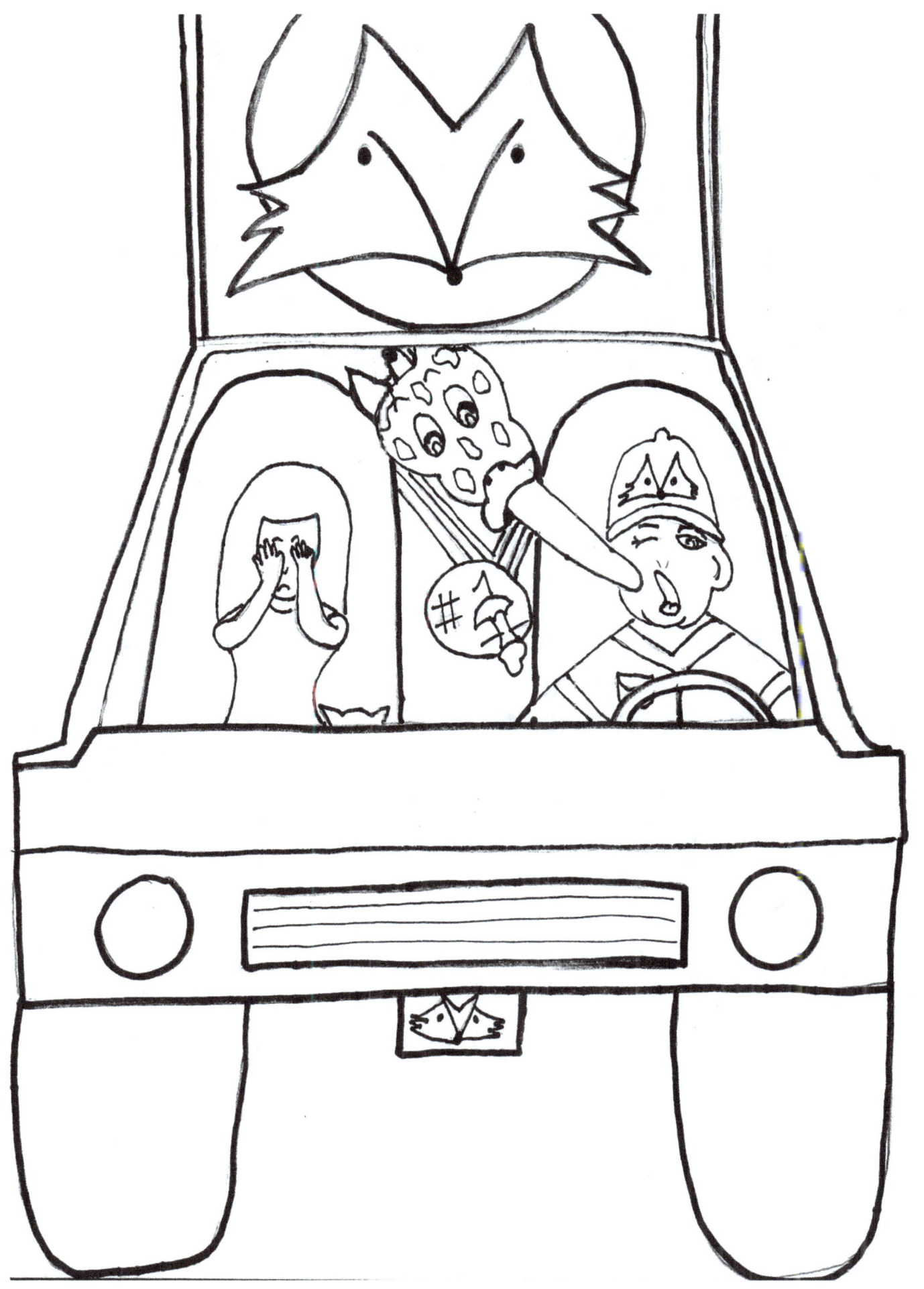

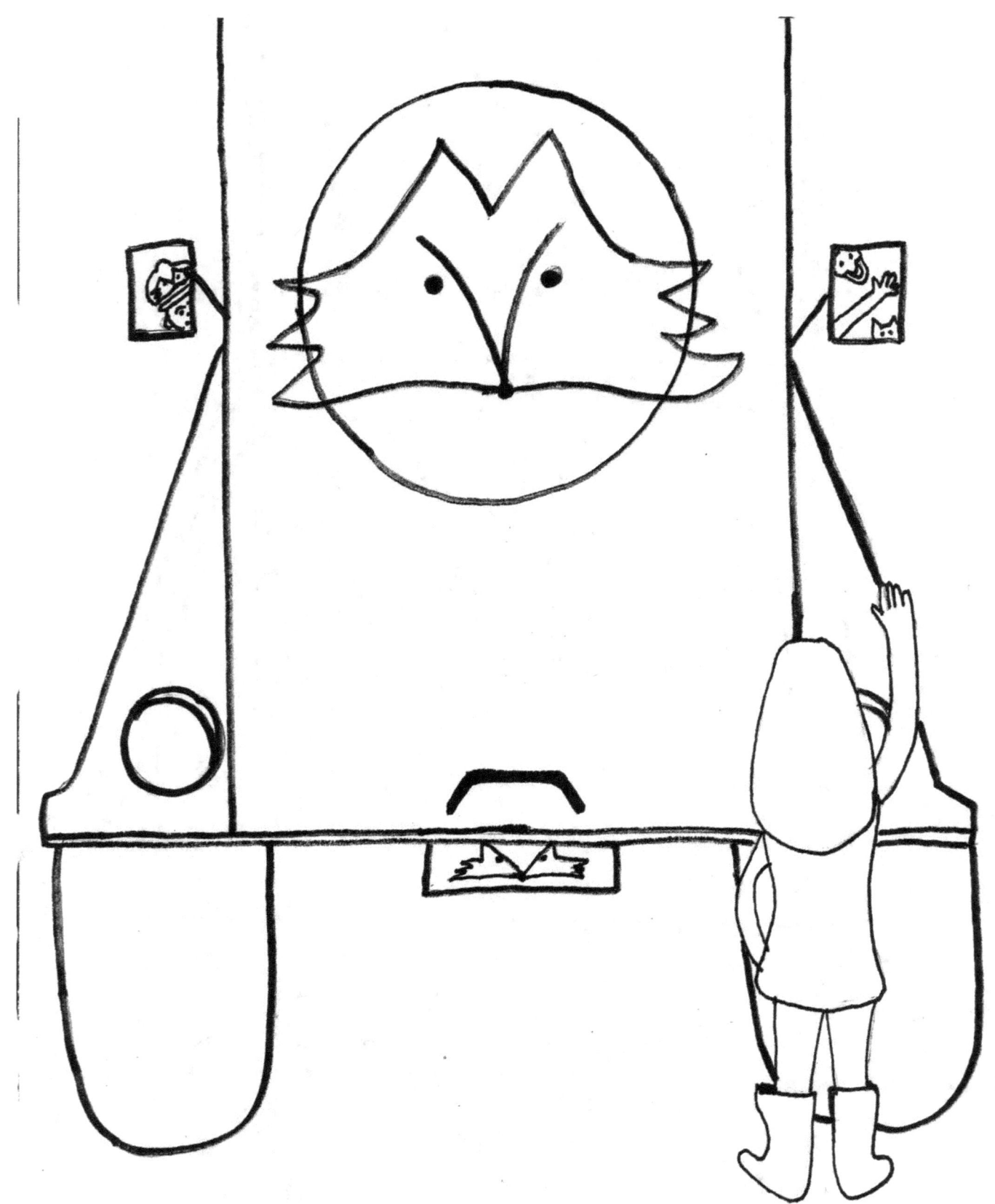

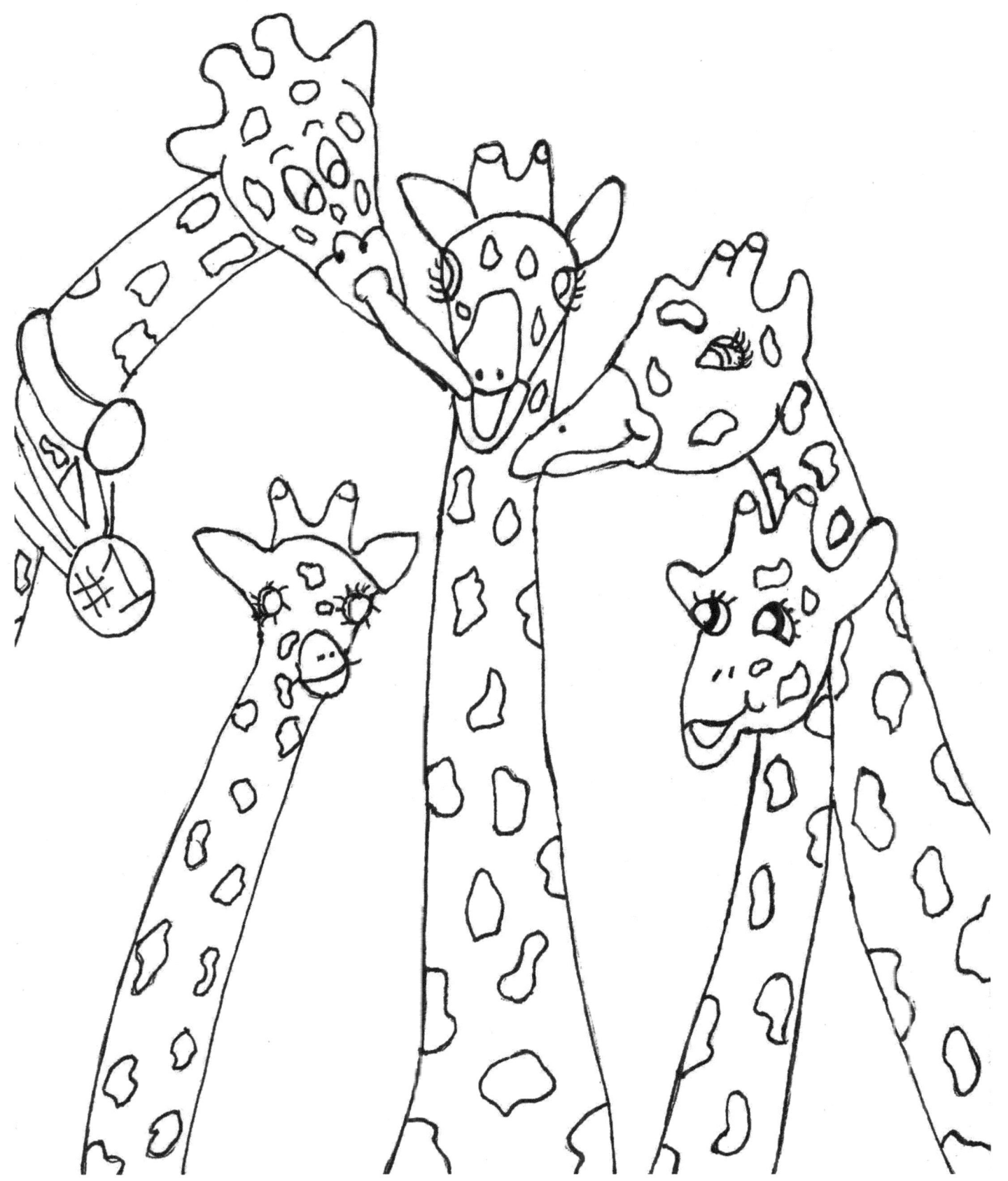

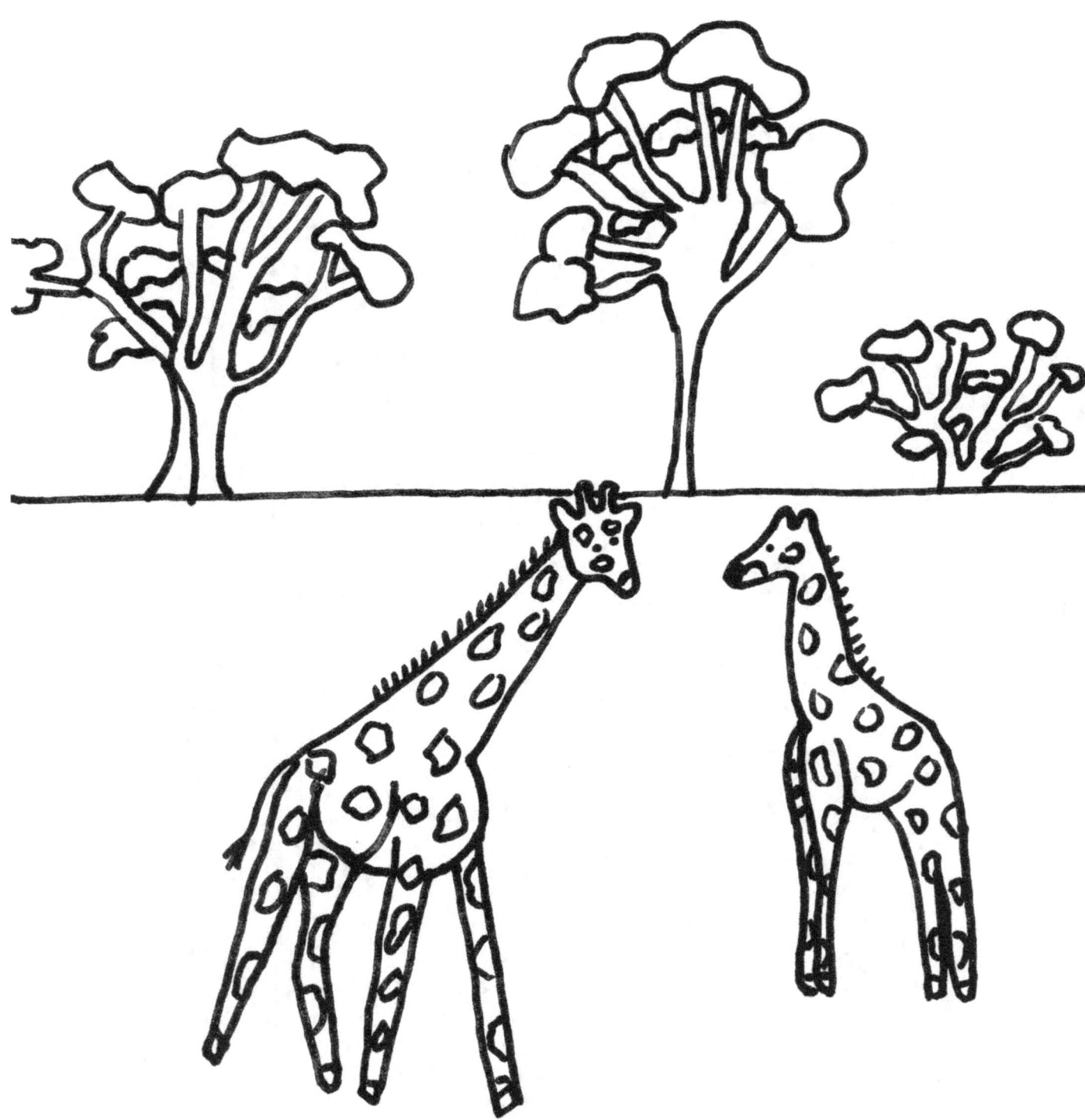

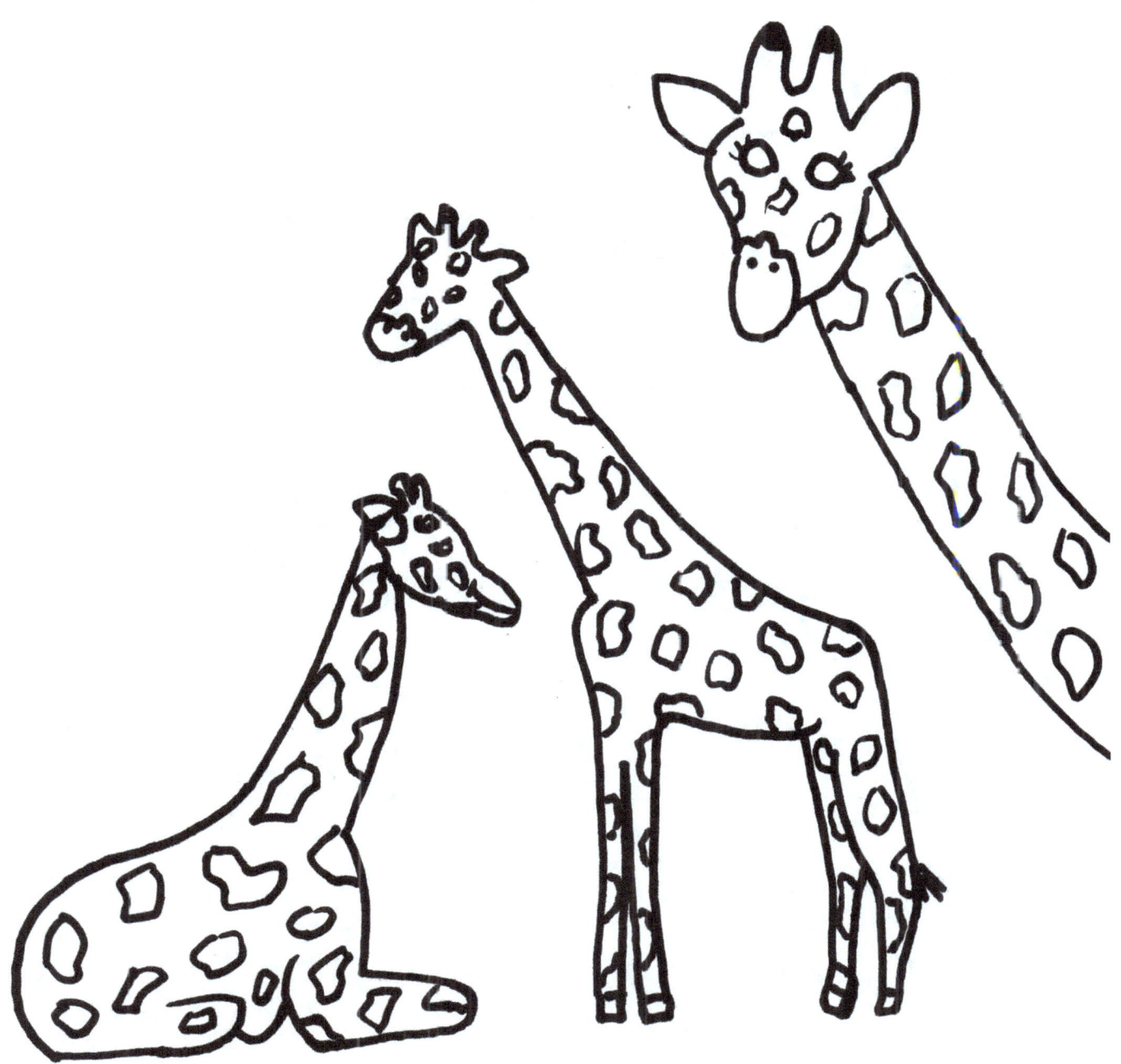

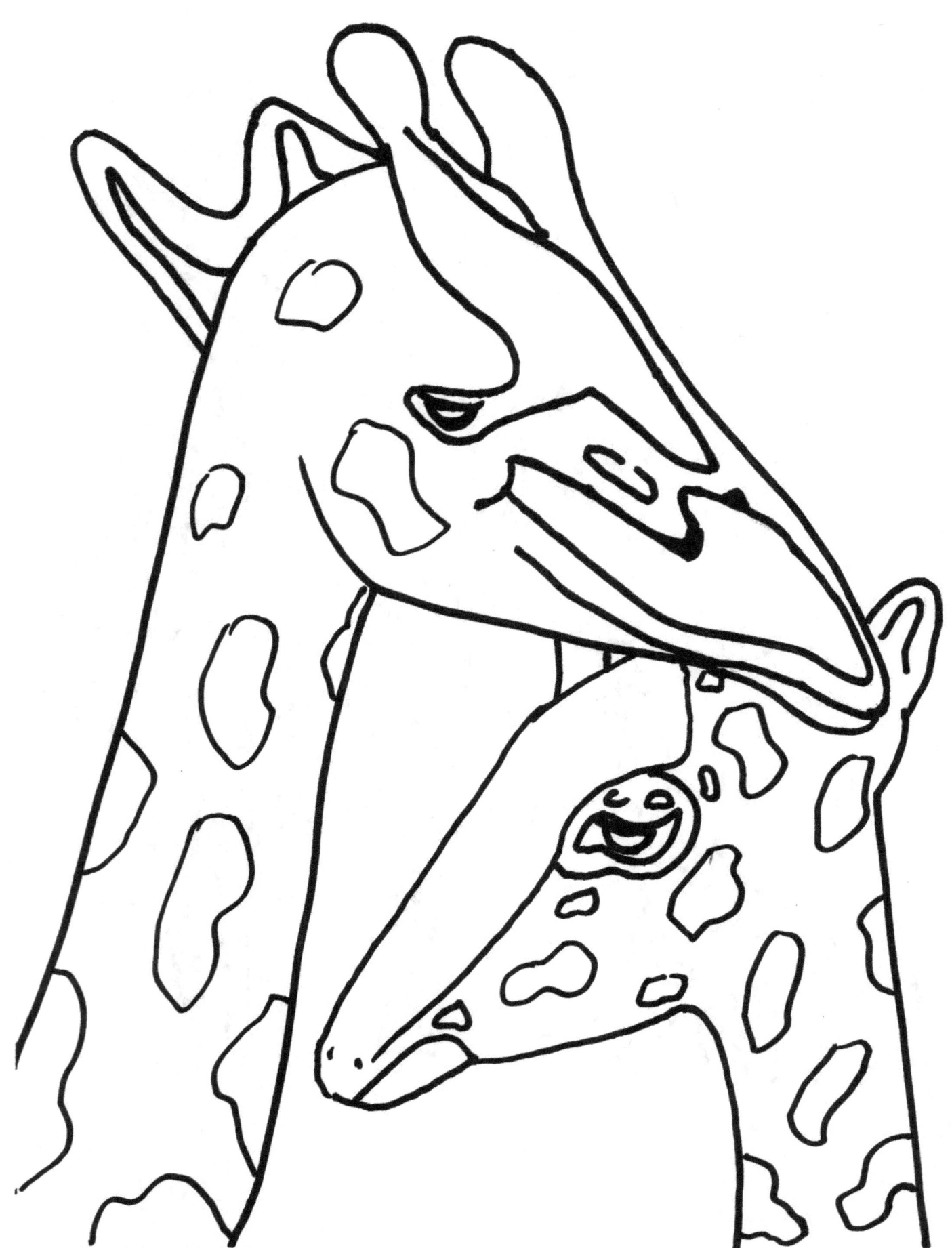

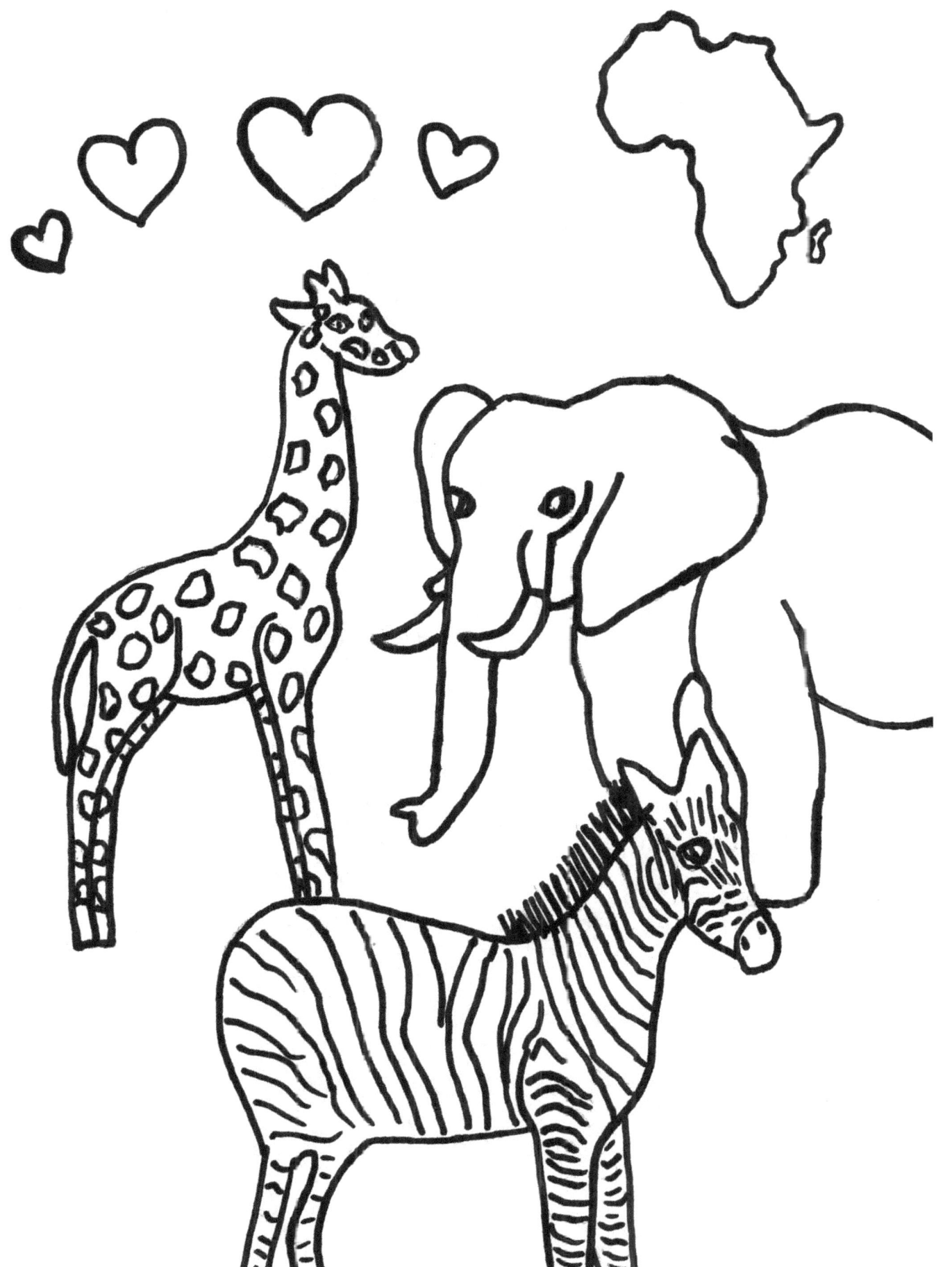

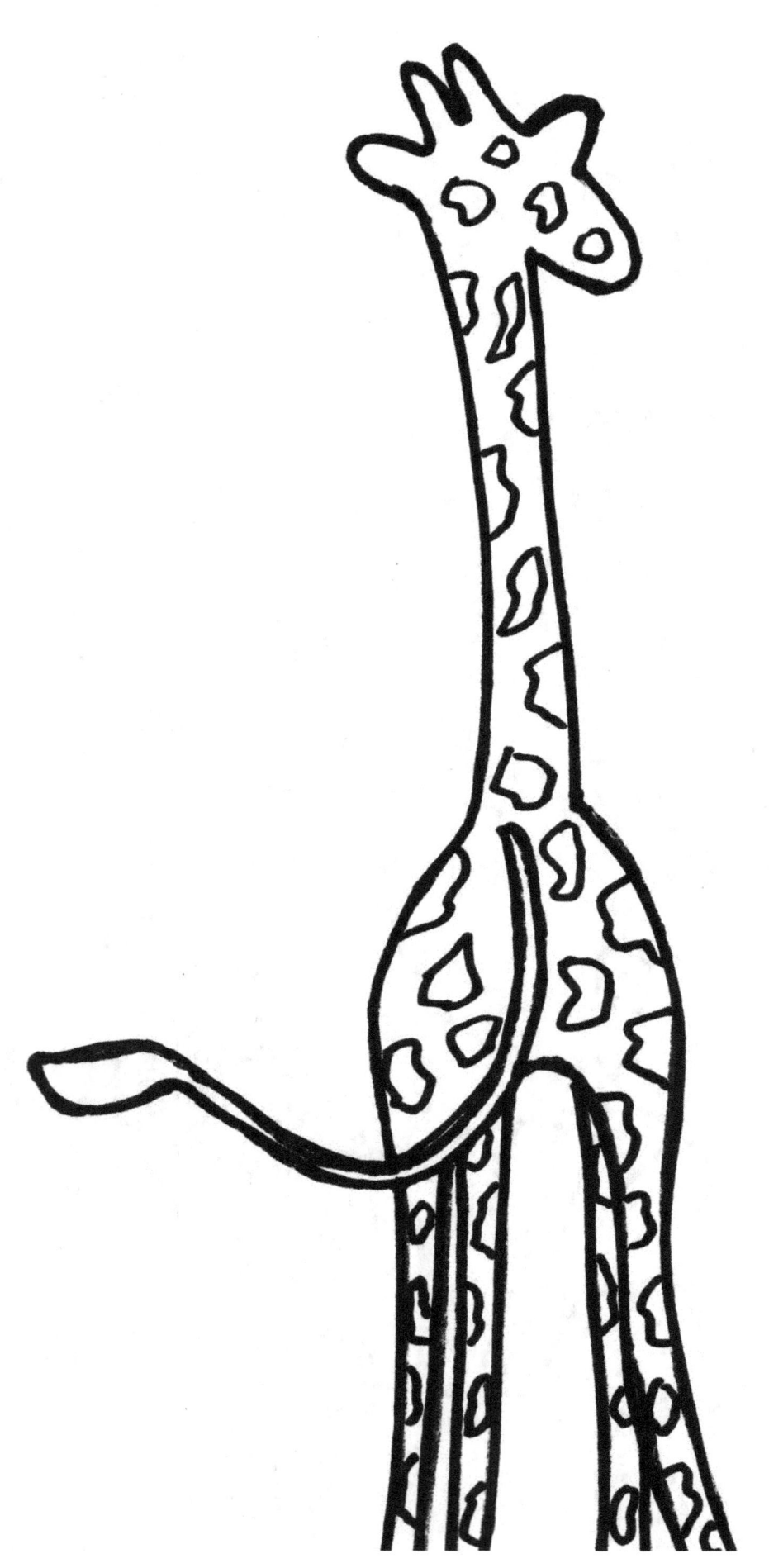

About the Author

K.C. Gardner resides in Southern California with her dog, Sugar Puppy. She is the doting aunt of three young nephews. K.C. has a variety of interests including, but not limited to: writing, drawing, photography, painting, running, roller skating and gymnastics. K.C. has spent the majority of her adult life as a preschool teacher. She loves children and animals. You can be sure she'll be writing more books featuring both!

Follow her on Facebook:
K.C.Gardner@KCkidatheart

Books by K.C Gardner, available on Amazon:

"I Got You an Elephant for Christmas!"

"Mr. Elephant and Sugar Puppy Coloring Book"

"Mr. Longneck's Escapade"

"Mr. Longneck" (Coloring Book)